Circus Towne

40 Acres of Fun and Fantasy

By
Veronica Francis

Anne,
Enjoy & Keep Laughing!

Ronnie

Table of Contents

Chapter 1: NH or Bust

It was March 30, 1972, when our Winnebago pulled into the Northlander Motel in Twin Mountain, New Hampshire. There seemed to be more trees than people around. Little did I know that within those trees, in my near future, a circus would appear.

"Here we are, kid, your new home!" my Dad beamed. My older sisters were wailing. They were 13 and 15 and just realized we moved from hip Long Branch, New Jersey to the rustic White Mountains of NH. I just turned seven and thought we were going on vacation. But no, we were here to stay.

My parents grew up on the New Jersey Shore. As they say, "the real one". They lived the life of long beach days, rides on the Pier, and country club dances. Then, at age 42 they'd had enough. It was 1972 and a rough time for New Jersey beaches. My dad owned and managed the carnival games and rides on the Long Branch Pier, but times were tough from 1969-72. Riots were erupting, and it wasn't safe for kids. My sisters were getting held up in our ticket booth, and my mom had to keep a big German Shepard with her at all times. I was young when we moved to NH. So my memories of NJ are vague, but I do remember the rides and the dog.

Twin Mountain, New Hampshire is a small town located at the base of Mt Washington (population 400). Our property was located along busy Route 3, a "Scenic Byway of the White Mountains". We lived in the section of Twin Mountain referred to as "The Strip", located between Franconia Notch and Crawford Notch. Twin Mountain is along the Appalachian Trail attracting hikers and visitors from all over the world. "The Strip" consisted of many small, independent motels and restaurants. In 1973, there were over 200 motel rooms for rent in Twin Mountain. I lived in a tourist trap. Even with all these tourists around, there wasn't much for entertainment; the mountains and rivers were the main attractions.

Twin Mountain was always a tourist destination. From the late 1800s through the 1940s, trains brought visitors from Boston, New York and elsewhere to enjoy the fresh mountain air. Some of these travelers included my mother and her family, the Rawsons. Several of the Rawson clan (myself included) suffer from ragweed allergies and asthma. In 1924, my great-grandfather, Perry Rawson, ventured north to find a summer home where they all could breathe easy and enjoy the mountains. Bethlehem, NH – known as the cleanest air town east of the Mississippi – attracted him. Perry owned a small brokerage house on Wall Street and lived in Deal, New Jersey. In the late 1920s, he built a summer home in Bethlehem, NH with views of the White Mountains. It was here that my grandmother, mother and the whole family spent summer vacations and roller skated. Yes, roller skated.

My great-grandfather started ice skating in the 1920s in New York. He was a member of the NY Skating Club and spent many hours studying different skaters' techniques. He enjoyed ice skating dancing, and felt it could be translated to roller skating if the wheels were fixed right and the technique was taught properly. (Aim Out, Lean In.)

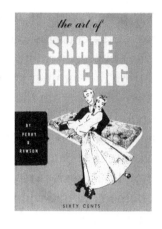

Perry became a leader in the roller skating community and even traveled to Europe to observe the latest skating strides. He developed his own technique for roller skating dancing and wrote books on the topic. Perry's roller skating books are still for sale today.

In his home in NJ and near the summer home in Bethlehem, he built roller skating rinks for the family. My mother and her cousins would practice roller skating dancing every day on their summer vacation and at the end of the summer, there would be a great performance for the neighborhood to enjoy. The audience was mostly family and friends, but they put on quite a show each year.

When I was growing up in New Jersey, our family visited Bethlehem every summer. So when the time came to move out of New Jersey, my parents knew right where they wanted to go. We moved to the town just up the river from Bethlehem: Twin Mountain, New Hampshire.

My parents bought 40 acres of land which came with a motel, 14 cottages, and a 3-bedroom home. The motel was open year-round; the little cottages were just open during the summer months. It was a traditional, roadside motel in the White Mountains; not a bed-and-breakfast. Nobody in my house could ever get up early and cook anyone breakfast, never mind feeding customers! But, the whole family jumped right into the motel business. My mom and sisters cleaned the rooms, I helped my dad run the front desk, and we all worked in the laundry room. Motel guests use numerous sheets and towels, resulting in a constant need for washing and folding. The front lobby always had that smell of a dryer. Even today when I smell a clothes dryer, I think of the Northlander Motel lobby.

We met so many interesting people at the motel. At seven years old, I was checking guests in and enjoyed talking to all the customers. This was in the 1970s, before computers or phones in the rooms. We just had stacks of registration cards behind the desk and a pay phone in the lobby. Coffee was only available if dad felt like making some. But people didn't come to the Northlander Motel for the amenities; they came for the Mountains.

You couldn't miss the White Mountains from any room in the motel. Mount Washington stands tall over the Town of Twin Mountain, while the Twin Mountains were right behind the motel. "The Twins" expanded across the skies in our backyard.

The land behind the motel was all forest, and it didn't take us kids long to figure out how to have fun on such expansive land. But to bring customers into a motel, you have to offer more than a forest. So, the first improvement my dad made to the motel was to install a swimming pool. The day the pool opened was one of the best days of my life, at least before the circus arrived.

Chapter 2: The Cement Pond

The Northlander Motel was a classic 1970s 10-room motel. We kept it clean and offered all the amenities that were popular at the time: a bed, bath and a TV with one channel. But starting in 1972, The Northlander Motel also featured a swimming pool! The first summer we were in NH, Dad installed an in-ground pool in the front yard - right on Route 3, the major highway Route through Twin Mountain. Our own pool, in the front yard! Big trucks would drive by and honk when you performed a funny dive off the diving board. It was a great platform for a ham like me.

We didn't care that the pool was for customers and that the family was supposed to share it with motel guests. That was just a minor inconvenience, we had a pool! I remember the day they came to build it. It was amazing to watch big, ugly bull dozers arrive, dig up the lawn, pour concrete, install blue tile and then fill it with water! To me, it was an oasis of 62-degree water with a diving board! This was before insurance companies scared away fun things such as diving boards. We learned how to dive, flip and do backward somersaults off that board. I cannon-balled over 100 times and drank gallons of chlorinated water during those summers.

I could always find Mom or my sisters during the summer afternoons at the pool. They would clean rooms in the morning and then hang out by the pool all afternoon. I was usually sent to get lunch at the snack bar next door. The grilled cheese sandwiches at that snack bar were family favorites. I would walk over to this funky red cottage where a woman named Jo had an antique shop and lunch grill. I would stand around in my bathing suit watching Jo cook our grilled cheese sandwiches on her big grill. She would tell me war stories of what life was like during World War II in Twin Mountain. Jo was a strong woman, and she liked to squish the sandwiches down with a big spatula to make very skinny grilled cheese. Until I was 25, I thought that all grilled cheese sandwiches were 1/8 inch thick. My mom would actually say "Ronnie, go get us some of Jo's squished grilled cheese sandwiches".

After watching and listening to Jo for almost an hour, I would walk back to the pool with brown lunch bags filled with grilled cheese sandwiches packed in wax paper. My bare feet would burn walking back to the pool on the hot pavement while my stomach growled with hunger. We would quickly gobble down those sandwiches to gear up for a whole afternoon of playing by the pool. Those squished grilled cheese sandwiches were so tasty - white bread, butter and American cheese! The way she squished those sandwiches made them taste even yummier. I'm not sure how she did it. I have tried over the years to squish my grilled cheese sandwiches like Jo used to, and have never been able to replicate that squish. But whenever I eat a grilled cheese, I always think of Jo and chlorinated water.

Chapter 3: The Back Lands

The land around the hotel seemed so expansive to me as
a little kid. The motel, cottages and house sat on about
two acres, the rest of the property was "out back". The
back land provided our family with lots of room for
activities and pets, which resulted in a lot of bruises. As
long as I can remember, my sisters always had horses.
Some women in our family have that "horse gene" that
affects about 70 percent of women nationwide (not a
statistical fact, just my guess).

Horses are big animals that need a lot of food, two times
per day. They poop whenever and wherever they feel
like it and sometimes step on you and bite you. Horses
are very sensitive to emotions and can tell if you are
nervous around them. I tolerate them, but that is not
enough. They want me to be strong and boss them
around like my sisters do. That does not happen. I just
try to sneak by, but that never works. The horses always
nudge me along with their big noses and show me who
is boss. Even when I agree with them, that they are the
boss, they are still not happy. They still demand more
food or blow a big raspberry in your face. It's in the
genes; you either get it or you don't. My grandmother
had it, my mom has it, my sisters caught it, and now my
niece has an irrational love of horses. It can skip
generations, and I'm so glad it skipped me so I do not
have to shovel horse poop every day.

But the horses were just the start to our circus life because life with a horse in your backyard can quickly turn into a circus. I was little when we lived in NJ, but I remember the hectic day when my sister's horse broke loose and ran down the Garden State Parkway. My whole family was chasing the horse in our big station wagon. The kids were all yelling at the horse to stop, and my mom tried to drive ahead of the animal. My family still tells the story of how the horse galloped right off the right exit and headed back to the barn!

When we moved from New Jersey to New Hampshire, we brought our two horses with us, and they were soon running around Twin Mountain. At our house, the horses were my first introduction to chaotic, funny madness. It was indicative of times to come with the circus.

Me, in front, and my friend, Anne,
riding Maranda, the horse we brought from NJ.
You can tell I'm not pleased about being on a horse.

Circuses have featured horses since ancient Rome. Early circus performances were mostly demonstrations of equestrian skills. To this day, you'll usually see a horse in the circus. But enough about the horses! We had more than enough land to play on; the horses only took up a small percentage.

The "back land" had a gravel pit, a stream, and a major snowmobile trail that ran right through the property. The back land provided nice hide-away spots for the whole family. The land seemed to go on forever. Our land just ran into our neighbor's land, where they also had acreage, snowmobile trails, and a gravel pit! Most of the land in Twin Mountain is either snowmobile trails or gravel pits; after all, NH is the granite state! The hills in a natural gravel pit can offer hours of entertainment. I sledded, skied, snowmobiled, and chased a lot of boys around on those hills for many years.

The five wooded acres next to our motel along busy Route 3 was prime land for an attraction. We needed some activity for all of the visitors staying in those motel rooms. Dad got bored within a year of renting rooms. Really how exciting is that for an Army guy, newspaper man and entrepreneur? Dad was always looking for a new business opportunity. He knew the carnival rides and games business from the Long Branch Pier, but "Spin Art" wasn't a real draw in Twin Mountain. No one even knew what it was! But Dad knew in his heart that games were always popular, and it just so happened that an "amusement guy" owned the campground down the street. These two entrepreneurs put their heads together and came up with an attraction to put Twin Mountain on the map....Circus Towne!

Chapter 4: The Circus Comes To Town

In the spring of 1973, excavation started on the land next to our motel. Dad and his new partner planned and financed a new tourist attraction, Circus Towne.

Circus Towne featured a traditional, live circus performance with wild animals, trapeze artists and clowns. Live circus acts performed 4 times per day, 7 days per week. A 7000 square foot concrete building was erected to feature a gift shop and a circus museum.

The museum featured a complete hand-carved miniature circus, "The Dickey Circus and Museum of Art". This miniature circus originated with the Late William T. Dickey, who started carving at the age of 12 in 1916. He spent over 10,000 hours carving with "Barlow pocket knives". This collection was modeled after the *John Robinson Circus* of the 1920s.

MASTER CARVER — A former resident of 725 Russell St., Bristol Virginia, W. T. Dickey, a man with a penchant for wood craving, will have portions of his hand carved scale model circus displayed at the National Hobby Hall of Fame in Cape Coral Garden, Fla. Dickey is shown pointing out details of his 1/12th scale circus wagons to Mrs. Betty Oesher, right, of the National Hobby Institute. Mrs. Dickey, left, looks on. The Dickey's now reside in Ft. Myers, Fla.

This miniature circus was displayed in a glass case, in one big huge room, the size of a bowling alley. The room was filled with miniature carvings of a complete circus including people, animals, structures, and tents. Word got out on the national "circus network" about Circus Towne, and we received circus artifacts from all over the country to display in the circus museum. The room was full of clown paintings, circus memorabilia, clown dolls, and some strange items that are still unidentifiable at this time.

The front of the main building was the entrance to the park, with a ticket booth and a large circus gift shop. Outside featured a live petting zoo with an elephant and pony rides. There was a ferris wheel, moon bounce and other kiddie rides. The big top tent out back was where the circus performance was held – rain or shine – four times per day. The *International All-Star Circus* from Sarasota, Florida agreed to spend the summer in New Hampshire and perform four shows every day. I'm not sure what the exact cost was to move a complete circus company to Northern New Hampshire, but somehow my dad and his partner found a way to finance it and to contract this professional circus company for the summer.

I remember the day the big top was installed. Every teenage boy in town (all 12 of them) showed up that day to erect the 110' round big top tent. The tent had one 50-foot center section and two 40-foot center poles. The seats were custom made and purchased from "Circus Bartok", a popular east coast 1970s circus company. It took the whole town to get that tent up and straight. The big top tent had seen better days and featured lots of holes for "sunlight". Well, when it rained hard, that tent did not stop much of it, and it seemed to have rained a lot that summer, usually around 7 pm when the nightly show started.

Now I was only eight years old when the traveling circus moved into my back yard. Even at that age, I could tell these were some interesting characters! Somehow they managed to fit into Twin Mountain. With all the tourists, locals, hikers, and our family, it really wasn't a stretch. I thought this was the best neighbor anyone could have and eagerly jumped into the circus life. (What do you expect? I was eight, and there was a live circus in my backyard!)

The circus company was a traditional, traveling circus show with performers from all over the world, and each performer agreed to work this gig for the summer. The shows included a leopard act, magicians, clowns, trapeze artists, tight-rope walkers, chimpanzees, elephants and even a gorilla show. It was a true 1973 circus complete with popcorn and loud canopy music. Let's just say, I didn't sleep much that summer.

Chapter 5: Clowning Around

Every circus has a clown, at least one. Clowns are a
vital part of circus history, as much as horses. At
Circus Towne, we had one boss clown and then a few
sidekicks or "augustes" and some extras. The extras
were the locals, including my sister and her friends
riding their horses in the finale.

The first year, the lead clown was billed as "Popcorn the
Clown". He wore the classic clown outfit with red curly
wig, white painted face with big red lips, funny circus
pants and big floppy shoes. He did the usual tricks,
juggled, pulled quarters out of your ears, and always had
a can of rubber snakes on hand.

Popcorn The Clown

Clowning around is a true art. On stage, Popcorn was a talented clown. Off-hours he was a thirty something angst-ridden guy who always looked sad. I worried about Popcorn. He would stop over now and then to see my dad and always looked like a despondent guy, but when Popcorn put on that costume, he was a true clown and determined to get a laugh.

Clowns always need a straight man. Every show they would pick an eager kid out of the audience to help them with a trick, but during slow shows, with only a few shy brats in the audience, they would pick me out of the audience to help out. I was a good sidekick. I watched the show every day, at least three times a day for 100 days; so I knew it by heart. But when I would get picked to come out of the bleachers and into the ring, it was a whole different view, and I loved it. I always acted surprised and laughed when appropriate. I remember once when I was really getting into the act and creating my own laughs from the audience, the clown I was helping said, "Hey, kid, don't steal all my laughs". I learned then that sidekicks are just that, on the side laughing, not creating the laughs.

Me and Toby the Clown
clowning around

The second year at Circus Towne, Popcorn the Clown
didn't return. That summer, we featured Buck, the
world's tallest clown! Buck the Clown was tall, 7'4"
and I was 4'8" back then. So he was definitely a long
way up to talk to. Buck was a professional. He didn't
need any sidekicks for jokes; he was the joke.

Buck the Clown took his art seriously. At my dad's
birthday party, he wanted to throw a pie in my dad's
face. I was, of course, very excited about this activity.
Before the party, Buck instructed me on the exact way to
prepare a whipped cream pie made exclusively for
throwing in a face. There is an exact twist of the hand to
twirl a pie plate so you do not hurt your victim. (Old
clown secret.) He also demonstrated how to hold the
neck with your left hand and bring the pie in with the
right. This way you prevent the victim from snapping
back his neck. I appreciated this technique since he was
preparing to smack my dad in the face with a whipped
cream pie! The party was a big success, and Buck
delivered the pie with grace and accuracy.

Buck the Clown was a friendly, talented clown. He
worked for many different circus companies for 33 years
and passed away in Virginia in 2004. Buck seemed to
enjoy being in Twin Mountain for that summer and got
along well with the locals. I always would know when
Buck was at the door of our house. He would ring the
doorbell, and one of us kids would pull back the curtain
to see who it was, and we would be eye level with his
belly button.

The "boss clown" for Circus Towne was Jim, the ring master and manager of the company: Jim's clown act was performed on the trampoline. He would do a few flips and some stunts getting his feet all tangled in the springs on the edges of the trampoline. It was always a hit. He made it look easy and taught me a few trampoline tricks so I could impress my friends. I learned fast that the goofiest tricks are really the hardest to perform.

Jim was the owner/manager of the *International All Star Circus* and responsible for keeping all the performers paid and in-line. At the time I didn't appreciate how hard that job must have been. I thought he had the best job in the world, The Ringmaster! He got to use the microphone and announce "*sit back, relax, and enjoy the fun and fantasy for the very young of heart*" and would announce the acts, four times per day, seven days a week. Now what job could be better than that? I thought I found my life's calling.

Chapter 6: Acrobatics – Don't Try This At Home

The most underappreciated, yet most astonishing, acts to watch every day were the tightrope walkers and the trapeze artists.

Today when you watch acrobatic acts, you see safety experts, ropes and nets all around. But when I watched Craig Carlson walk up that wire to the top of the big tent, without a very big net below, I knew all he had to keep him alive was his balance and skill. He walked up a cable from the ground to the top of the rickety tent, held together with steel rods a few local guys had installed that Spring. The same local guys who could barely fix my mom's brakes. These are not safety experts! It was a real life- risking act performed every day to earn a living. In the first year of Circus Town, we had a tightrope walker (who also juggled fire), a couple who did rope tricks and a Mexican trapeze artist.
The couple who performed the rope trick would hang each other by the neck from a rope in the middle of the tent and spin each other. They would wrap their arms and legs around that rope and twirl. Their big act was "The Spin". This was a trick where the guy would wrap the rope around his wife's neck like a noose and then proceed to spin her really fast. It was cool to watch, but that poor woman always looked dizzy and had blood shot eyes. The rope couple was quiet and didn't mingle much with the other performers. I only saw them when they were practicing or waiting for the next show backstage. They always had rope burns on their arms and legs. I decided then that rope twirling was not a career I would pursue.

After the tightrope walker, the next big act at Circus Towne was La Chona, the trapeze artist. A beautiful, Mexican woman who could flip and swing and float in the air effortlessly, she performed four times per day, seven days per week. She rode a unicycle back and forth on a wire, with no net below her. La Chona's famous act was balancing on a chair on the trapeze, *sans* net. She would happily swing from her trapeze, hanging from the old tattered tent that the locals installed. She would flip and hang from one foot on the bar, with no net, just her husband running back and forth below her ready to catch her if she fell. Luckily we never saw him have to catch her, except in practices when they would try new tricks.

She was a true professional, and I admired her so. I wanted to wear sequined bikinis and swing from a trapeze all day. Luckily, she set me straight about the realities of life in the circus. She sat me down one day, fed me the most delicious egg sandwich while she told me the history of Mexican trapeze artists and how tough it was living with the circus. She told me about the Flying Codonas, a popular Mexican trapeze artist family who suffered fatal deaths and suicides during the early 1900s. She forcefully expressed that the circus was not an easy life and to not make it a career choice. This was an important bit of advice for me, since I had the application to circus college all completed at age 8.

The trapeze wasn't La Chona's only gig. She also performed a trained gorilla act, "Congo the Almost Human Gorilla". (Congo was her husband dressed up as a gorilla.) She would enter the ring to loud jungle music, carrying a whip and wearing a zebra print bikini. She had the biggest boobs I had seen since we left the Jersey Shore. She'd crack that whip and really pretend that she was training that gorilla. The gorilla costume was well made, and most kids thought it was a real gorilla. La Chona would have the gorilla perform a few tricks, jump through a hoop or do a somersault. But then the gorilla would become agitated and would start to get rowdy. He would run around the ring and not listen to the trainer. La Chona would look panicked and start to really yell at the Gorilla. He would then run up into the bleachers and start to tickle an audience member. This is where our circus got interactive. He would goof with a kid or sit on a guy's lap. Audience members by then were all laughing and screaming. The gorilla would then find an innocent looking, bored woman sitting alone (who was planted in the audience every night) and proceed to flirt with her. After tormenting the woman for a few minutes, he would then steal her purse. He would grab it and sit down in the bleachers to investigate this purse. He would rummage through it, pulling out embarrassing items while the woman screamed in panic. There was always a bra in the purse, and the gorilla would try wearing it on his head. That trick always got a good laugh. (It often made me wonder if all women carried a spare bra in their pocketbook. Is that why handbags are so big? I later realized in life, once I started wearing a bra and carrying a purse, not many of us carry a spare bra around.)

Anyway, the gorilla act always got a loud applause. The woman planted in the audience was usually a friend of the family, a local woman who enjoyed being part of the show. My mom's friend, El, was one of the best at looking surprised and scared. She was so good at acting that one night when she was in the audience pretending to be a spectator, my dad didn't even recognize her.

Me being attacked by the gorilla

We all got into show business that summer. My sister and I ran the spotlight for many performances. We learned the sequence for changing the colored lights along with the music and when not to shine the light in the trapeze artist eyes. Mostly we just pointed the spotlight at the center ring. It was quite the demanding job; one of us had to be there to keep the lights on for every show, every day, for $5/week. I was usually there hanging around the shows anyway, either in front of or behind the spotlight. I loved the spotlight. My friends will tell you I still look for it any chance I get.

Chapter 7: Magic Acts

There was one couple, Heinz and Patty, who had four acts between them. That is what you call job security! Every day they performed a ventriloquist act, a leopard show with flames, a magic act and foot juggling. It was the foot juggling that I was really drawn to.

Patty would wear fishnet stockings (a very popular garment in 1970 circuses) and lie on her back; legs extended, and proceed to juggle large round objects with her feet. This act inspired me to spend many hours on my couch with feet in the air, juggling the  plastic bathroom garbage can. I could go 20 seconds before it crashed into something. For a couch potato like me, this seemed to be a great career choice!

Targa, the spotted African leopard that jumped through hoops of fire, was exciting to watch perform, but he wasn't very friendly. And I never really got too close with that cat; he always eyed me like a piece of meat.

Then there was the ventriloquist act. I watched it so many times, I knew every word by heart. I didn't really know I knew it all by heart until one night at a party at our house. It was my dad's birthday in July, and all the circus people came over for a rare visit to our home. I remember the drinks were flowing, and everyone was in a good mood. I was upstairs in my room when they called me down to the living room. I was excited to be in front of all the performers I watched every day. They egged me on to sit on Heinz's lap and play the part of the dummy. I went along and mouthed all the dummies responses easily and on queue. I enjoyed entertaining all the performers who entertain so many every day. They got a kick out of this party trick, and it was repeated a few times over the summer. I bet Heinz got a chuckle out of some kid knowing his act as well as he did.

Heinz and Patty were multi-taskers before that was even a word. They had the leopard act, magic act, juggling with fire and foot juggling, but The Box Trick was their main gig. It amazed us all, and my mom still talks about how they did it to this day. It was an amazing trick, one of those illusion acts where they lock the woman in the box, tie chains around it to secure it and then she appears outside the box in an instant. It baffled us for weeks. We knew there was a sneaky trick to how she did it, but they would never tell. It was finally revealed to us one slow night by accident. It was an awkward performance that night, and they covered it up as professional performers do. Heinz took our eyes off the box while someone else helped Patty, but we professional circus spectators saw it all happen and realized the trick. It was like learning the truth about the Easter Bunny. You still enjoy Easter, but it loses a little of the magic.

Chapter 8: Chimps, poodles & elephants, oh my!

What would a circus be without an elephant? The International All Star Circus featured Mike Rice and his three performing elephants, Whimpy, Rajah and Chang. It was the first time I had ever touched an elephant. I had seen them at zoos, but that summer we rode the elephants. I preferred riding elephants over horses – it is hard to ride a horse by just holding its ears.

There was plenty of excitement in New Hampshire when the elephants arrived. On their way from Florida, Mike stopped at a motel in Massachusetts and let the elephants lounge outside his room, taking a break from the road. Apparently the elephants decided to take a walk around town, and they proceeded to leave the motel grounds. Word got out fast about elephants on the loose! Soon police cars and even helicopters were circling the suburbs of Massachusetts chasing down the missing elephants. Whimpy, Rajah and Chang were soon returned to the hotel, but made their presence known to all of New England. The story appeared in all the newspapers that week.

ENJOYED SHORT-LIVED FREEDOM — After enjoying 18 hours of freedom, pre-cocious pachyderms — who went for a romp in the woods of Shrewsbury — are led back to their trailer by owner Michael Rice. The elephants had broken away out of the vehicle and went wandering in the woods until their capture. They're presently en route to a New Hampshire amusement park. (AP)

Elephant rides were a popular attraction in Twin Mountain. I was fortunate by my close proximity to Circus Towne to be able to enjoy many elephant rides during the slow days. I would gallop along the snowmobile trail holding on to those ears with all my kid strength. I don't recall any abuse to these elephants, except, of course, being sentenced to life in a circus. These elephants were healthy and didn't look too sad.

Not like the chimpanzee! The main chimp in the show was mean and disliked his job. He would constantly be screaming from his cage, so much so that we would often hear his owner, Mr. T, shoot a gun in the air to quiet the chimp down. We'd be playing around by the pool in front of the motel and hear gun shots. My mom would say "I guess Mr. T is practicing his show again". The chimp would perform his act every day and was pretty well-behaved in front of an audience. The chimp was nice to me, but he didn't like to be alone with Mr. T. No one liked to be alone with Mr. T.

One day my mother and I were walking down the Main Street of Littleton, doing some shopping, when we heard a horrible scream. We looked around to see what the noise was, and here comes Mr. T's truck, rocking and rolling with the mean chimp in the back shaking the trailer and screaming. I guess Mr. T. needed to go shopping as well, and had to take his traveling animals with him wherever he went. I can't remember much about that act; I just mostly remember the chimpanzee screaming in Mr. T's truck. But the chimpanzee wasn't the only animal that lived in Mr. T's trailer. He also had a poodle act, which was really poodle mayhem. It was a funny dog act with 12 poodles running in a circle and jumping through hoops. It was fun to watch the poodles running around aimlessly, peeing on the circus poles while Mr. T. yelled at them. That guy must have spent his best years yelling at that chimp and the poodles. Mr. T. only lived one summer in Twin Mountain, and I wonder how long that act lasted. I haven't seen a live screaming chimpanzee on Main Street, Littleton since.

It was only during the first year of Circus Towne that we featured wild animals in the circus. There was Targa, the spotted African leopard that jumped through hoops of fire. You don't see many of those in the White Mountains!

As traditional circus professionals know, the more animals you have, the stronger the circus. The second and third year didn't feature any wild animals, and the circus just wasn't the same.

My dad tried to keep the animal spirit alive by having a petting zoo in the main area of Circus Towne. Now, as I mentioned, my dad always looked for opportunities. If we couldn't have animals performing in the circus (too expensive), Dad wanted animals in a petting zoo for kids to play with. But where does one find these animals?

At an animal auction in Vermont, of course. So the next spring, we traveled two hours in the back of a truck to buy some animals for the petting zoo. This animal auction mostly sold cows for farmers (it was Vermont), but somehow I ended up riding home in the back of the truck with miniature goats and sheep to fill the pens at Circus Towne.

To keep the tourists entertained, my dad also landed some funny monkeys to live in the petting zoo. He built these wire cages with domes on top. The domes were shaped like mushroom caps and painted in bright colors. The cages were built specifically for the monkeys to be comfortable in and featured a coin-operated feeder, so kids could feed the monkey for just a nickel. The monkeys were not very friendly, and by the end of the summer, they were tired of kids and the cheap grain in that machine. So one day a monkey bit a young girl visiting the circus. Oh boy, that was big news all over town, and we had to rush her to the hospital for stitches. Twin Mountain didn't have an ambulance service at that time, so my dad had to drive her 20 minutes to the hospital. For some reason, after biting that brat, the monkey died. I wasn't surprised because I never really liked that girl, but the hospital was concerned about rabies and wanted that monkey tested. By now, the monkey is dead, and the lab is two hours away. The hospital told us to keep him frozen until he was picked up by officials. One of the helpful Circus Towne employees placed the dead monkey in the freezer, which seemed like a good idea until the soda salesman came in to check the cooler and came face-to-face with the dead monkey. Needless to say, that was the end of monkeys in the petting zoo.

But we had those cool cages with domes that needed something in them for the kids to feed. So the next year, when we were heading back to the animal auction, my sister came up with the great idea that a turkey would fit in the cage and could be the new attraction. A few hours later, I was riding home from Vermont in the back of a van with Milton the Turkey. He did turn out to be interesting to look at, and he really liked the cheap grain from the five-cent feeder machine. But again, by Labor Day, he was tired of smiling at tourists and started snipping at kids. Nothing that broke any skin, but let's just say that with Thanksgiving around the corner, Milton didn't get his contact renewed and was sold off to the local restaurant. A few days after Thanksgiving, we heard from the owner of the restaurant that Milton was supposed to be the main meal on the holiday menu, but when they went to carve the bird, they found him tough as nails from eating all the junk food the kids fed him over the summer. That ended the turkey petting zoo, and we moved on to rabbits. Rabbits eat cheap grain, live for years, and don't bite kids too hard.

To go along with the petting zoo and the circus theme, my mother thought to dress me up as a clown and walk a pig on a leash around the park. That was my job for the summer. We bought a little pig, named it Petunia, and she actually lived in our house for a while. Pigs can be housebroken!

Each day, I would dress up with the full make-up, a funny wig, a cute clown outfit and take the little pig for walks around the park just to make people laugh. It was a funny sight, but at the end of the summer, when the pig got sold to the same local restaurant, I didn't think it was so funny anymore. Poor Petunia; I went on to 5th grade, and she ended up in the freezer. That experience didn't sit well with me. I gave up my clown shoes and leash after that summer.

The petting zoo ended a few years after the circus, as well as the trips to the Vermont Auction. I didn't miss those goats always trying to buck me with their horns or the sheep baahhhhing all day, but it seemed when the animals went, so did the circus.

Chapter 9: Bad Acts

The first two years of Circus Towne featured a professional circus company from Florida. By the third year, things started to get a little sketchy. The third year was the summer of '75. The economy was not doing great, and the northern NH winters proved to be a very long time in between the Circus Summer seasons. My dad's partner couldn't stand it; he packed up the winter of '75 and moved to Florida. He left Dad with all the debt, no contracts and this 6000 square foot concrete building with nothing in it except clown memorabilia. The miniature circus museum moved out; the big tent was taken down, and all that was left was a big, rectangular, concrete building with pavement around it and deep holes in it showing where the rings once stood. But not being a quitter, my dad stood strong and contacted the circus people he knew to find us acts for the next summer season. I'm not sure where he found these guys, but they were considered a "medicine show". They dressed as weird chemists and would perform a funny act creating concoctions that would blow up in their faces. I remember the organ player behind the stage. He was odd. He would stay behind the scenes and play low, dramatic chords for the act. I have a creepy memory of one day when he wanted to show me how to play the organ, back in his trailer. I got the feeling that the organ he was referring to wasn't the keyboard. I graciously declined and ran home fast.

The acrobatic act that year was a family that consisted of a mother and four girls. The girls were talented gymnasts. They wore fishnet stockings and gold sequined body suits. Those outfits were hot! The mother sewed them all herself. These little girls were constantly doing cartwheels and flips all over the place. They all looked alike to me, petite southern blondes with perfect skin and smiles. They thought I was a diamond in the rough, with my messy hair and wrinkly clothes. One day, they talked me into a make-over. The acrobat girls fixed me all up with the up-hairdo, sequined body suit, fishnet stockings and high heels. I looked scary, and it felt like Halloween in July. The acrobat girls thought I finally looked normal, rather than the scruffy kid I usually was, but I couldn't keep up with their flips and jumps. That family lasted six weeks, and then moved on to the next town. They took all their sequins and fishnet stockings with them.

By this point, we were all beginning to think that circuses were going out of style. The acts and people just didn't have the same magic as the original circus company. In 1975, there was a popular circus taking off in San Francisco called "The Pickle Family Circus". We were more like the "Farkle Family Circus".

That summer of 1975 was when the "traditional circus" was falling out of style, but before the revival of the "contemporary circus" that came about in the 1980s introducing the new style of circus acts we see today in Las Vegas or Montreal. There is something about an old-fashion circus act. It can sweep you away into the magic of the show, even in a holey tent with one spotlight in a back parking lot. A professional circus brings out the kid in all of us, but not all acts do. That summer, my inner kid was scared. Scared of what was to come of this back lot with no real acts, scared of the energy crisis, and not sure what to think of Saturday Night Live and The Rocky Horror Picture Show, both of which premiered that summer. Humor was changing fast.

That summer was weird. We had the weird medicine show acts on the back lot, too many mean goats in the petting zoo, a snack bar where I ate over 100 fudgesicles to help alleviate my fear and a new attraction out front: go-karts. Since we didn't need so much parking anymore, my dad turned half of the parking lot into an oval go-kart racing track. Dad already knew the business from the Long Branch Pier in NJ and knew where to buy the go-karts.

Remember this is 1975; there were no helmets, and the chain-link fence that surrounded the track was only protected by bales of hay. These go-karts are not like the luxury ones you see today at amusement parks. These were dirty metal carts, a plastic seat a few inches off the ground with the engine wide open right behind your head. The go-kart track was a big hit in town. People came from all over the North Country to pay $2.00 to drive those carts around the driveway for 5 minutes. On Saturday nights, the lines were over 20 people long, but we always shut down by 10:00 pm to appease the neighbors.

Thank goodness those go-karts were popular! Those $2.00 ticket sales paid the debt left by the circus years. It is a tough business though; the karts often broke down, and someone was always getting hurt. I can remember a few gruesome scenes where someone would crash through the fence and scrape their face up. We soon realized the importance of an ambulance service. When we first arrived in town, one of our motel guests had an accident at the motel and broke his arm. My dad went to call the emergency number and was told there was no ambulance. The neighbors told him to get in his car and drive the guy to the local hospital, which was 20 minutes away in Littleton, NH. After many scary trips to the hospital, my dad and his friends rallied the money and training to install an ambulance/emergency volunteer service in Twin Mountain. Thanks to Dad and my uncle Mervin, Twin Mountain got a good deal on a used ambulance from our old neighborhood, Oakhurst, New Jersey. Twin Mountain really needed an ambulance after the go-karts came to town.

One day when I was hanging around, it was quiet, and the attendant was fixing a go-kart and testing it out. The attendants loved to ride the karts around the track while reaching around the back of the seat to flicker the carbonator to make it go faster. This guy was doing that when something went wrong, and he chopped off the top of his finger! He walked into the building and told the girls working the ticket booth. They screamed and got my dad, who, of course, drove him to the hospital. While the girls were screaming and the wounded guy was stumbling to the car, the other attendant ran in with the rest of his finger. He found it on the track. It was covered with oil. I couldn't help but look at it. It reminded me of a black olive. They took the finger and the patient to the hospital, but the top of the index finger could not be saved. He worked the rest of the summer with a bandage on that finger, and it was a good lesson to the rest of the guys on the track: don't stick your fingers too far in the engine when driving!

That guy who cut his finger visited a few years later, and he showed us all how his finger grew back. That was good to see. But those guys were always getting hurt. The attendants handled the obnoxious ladies who didn't know how to stop the carts and almost ran them down, the kid who thought it was funny not to stop and the constant engine trouble while lines of hyped-up customers were waiting to ride. The go-karts kept everyone busy that summer.

Chapter 10: Balls and Beer

By the summer of '76, Circus Towne was definitely old news. Only freaks and little kids wanted to go to a circus. Times were changing. That was a hot, dry summer, and the Summer Olympics were hosted only a few hours away in Montreal, Canada. It was the year Nadia Comaneci received perfect 10s and made me regret not paying more attention to those tricks the acrobat girls tried to teach me. The top songs that year included Abba and the Bee Gees. To keep up with the times, my dad dropped the whole circus vibe and changed the name of the business from Circus Towne to Fun Towne. All the fun you can have in the White Mountains of New Hampshire, with an "e"!

The go-kart track was still popular. To add more attractions for the same target audience, my dad installed a six-lane bowling alley and a bar, a perfect complement to men racing machines on pavement! But bowling was a big hit, and leagues became very popular in the 70s and 80s. So of course, our family became bowling enthusiasts!

The bowling alley fit perfectly in the big room where the miniature circus museum was. It was long with low ceilings. Bowling in New England means candlepin bowling, the little balls. You get 3 balls to a frame, and the deadwood stays lying near the other pins. So it is a little tricky to get high scores. Being from New Jersey, I never played candlepin bowling until the day the alleys opened at Fun Towne.

The lanes were all newly polished wood and the pins were bright white. The balls even shined. It was a whole new world for me at 12. I obviously had to start bowling at least 3 hours a day to be able to beat my friends easily.

But what is a bowling alley without a bar. Bowling is definitely more fun with a beer. (A fact I discovered a few years later.) But to own a bar in New Hampshire isn't easy. NH state liquor licensing laws are tough. NH does not have any sales or income tax. It is the "Live Free or Die" state, but it does have a liquor tax. Even with the tax, our liquor is still cheaper than in neighboring "Taxachusettes". But to obtain a license to serve liquor is not easy; to serve booze, a bar must serve food. Well, my dad didn't want to get into the restaurant business. He knew better. That is a tough business to own. He did find there was a bowling alley exception law for bars in New Hampshire that allows bowling alleys to serve liquor, without food but only 8-lane bowling alleys. We could only fit 6 lanes in the Fun Towne building. This was quite a setback for the business plan. I know my mom's cooking, and there was no way my parents could or should own a restaurant.

Well, we were in New Hampshire where politics is as much of a sport as deer hunting. The NH house of Representatives is made up of 400 members. These members are from all sections of New Hampshire, the cities in the south and the small towns around the lakes and mountains. There were always a few from the North Country, and these Representatives were always looking to bring a bill to the floor. An old NH law requires that all bills, no matter how wacky, go through a public hearing before there's a House vote. It is one of the reasons NH is so political. We are the first presidential primary state, we take politics seriously, and our representatives work hard for their $100/year.

So when the time came to open the bowling alley without a bar, my dad called our local state representative who lived in nearby Jefferson. She was a new congress person and eager to help. She drafted a bill that would allow a 6-lane bowling alley to operate a bar without serving food. The law passed and was dubbed the "Al Francis law". The community was spared my mother's cooking.

The bar opened in 1977 and quickly became the fun hangout for the locals. The counter in the bar was made from an old milled tree that was finished with the knots and lines still visible. There was a jukebox, a pool table, and the bar looked out through an 8-foot glass window onto the bowling alley. The window was the entertainment. One could sit there and watch people bowl through the glass, but not hear it, and the way it was situated, you couldn't see past the ball return; so you never knew what pins the player actually hit. You only could see the bowler run up to the line, toss the ball, and then watch their body language to tell if they hit a few pins or if they got a gutter ball. It was great entertainment, and it worked well for bowlers to wave at the people at the bar to tell them when it was their turn.

The Fun Towne bar and bowling alley livened up Twin Mountain in the 80s. This was the decade for excess, and even Twin Mountain was excessive. There were six bars just in Twin Mountain. Nearby Bethlehem and Franconia, two towns with a combined population of under 1000, had four bars each. Drinking and eating were the main industry in the area. We all worked in restaurants or motels and knew the value of tips! We also learned to drink. The drinking age was 18, which meant you could serve liquor at age 16. So I started bar tending as soon as I could and enjoyed the showmanship of the profession. It seemed just like performing in the circus, except drunks are more easily entertained!

The bowling and go-karts were going great, but we still had all that back land just sitting there. My dad had to think up some way to utilize that resource. The first few winters, he tried creating "Winter Wonderland". We rented snowmobiles with a guided tour and had an ice skating rink in the back lot where the circus tent was. Rental of snowmobiles and skates to tourists teaches one fast about the limits of the human brain. Those snowmobiles got cracked up pretty bad. It was quite the sight to see, one local guy being the leader, with ten snow machines behind him weaving and hitting trees.

The ice skating rink was a real hassle. It was one of the warmest winters on record, and we just didn't have the resources to keep an ice rink smooth. It was a bumpy rink, with a crackly speaker hung on the back of the building, blaring the local radio station. Not really Rockefeller Center. The locals tried it, but it really didn't catch on enough to sustain itself. I remember a lot of lonely nights ice skating by myself to the staticky radio.

The next summer, we tried roller skating. Now roller skating is an important sport in my family. As I mentioned before, my great-grandfather, Perry Rawson, championed the art of roller skating dancing in the 1930s. He was a real enthusiast about roller skating. Skating was a skill my mom and her cousins had to master during their visits to Perry's house. He taught them all to glide backwards and forwards gracefully with spins and kicks. So since roller skates were in our blood, it was a natural to try roller skating rentals on the back pavement, where the ice skating rink was. The same crackly speaker belted out popular 80s tunes, and we rented helmets, knee pads and skates to all who dared to try it. It was a little dangerous since the pavement had holes in it from where the big top tent spikes were, and it is a hard fall on asphalt! But folks tried it, and it did ok for a couple of summers but barely brought enough income to cover the cost of all those skates. So, back to the drawing board it was for my dad to come up with the right attraction. Since we had beer, bowling, and go-karts, the next new attraction in 1990 was golf. Miniature golf and a driving range were added to the land around the building, and it was a big hit. Mini golf is something tourists will always play when bored enough.

The driving range was popular for everyone but my family. We soon realized how many golf balls are needed to keep a range going in the busy times: hundreds of golf balls. I can still picture all those different colored balls in these big sinks in the club house. We had to wash every ball and then put them in buckets on the counter. The customers would then drive these balls 100-300 feet out into the back field. Then we had to go pick them all up, wash them and put them back in buckets for the next guy. This went on every day. There was no end to having to go "pick up the golf balls". It could be dangerous. I would be out picking up balls, and some golfers would start driving balls right at me! We had to start wearing helmets to protect us from stray balls flying above our heads. Not too long after we opened, dad bought a golf cart and rigged up a ball picker-upper thing that would drag behind the cart. This contraption saved us lots time and possible concussion. I never could get the hang of golf. I could putt, but could never drive very well. My friend told me it was because my boobs were too big and interfered with a proper swing. I took that as a good reason not to go into a career where I needed to play golf to get ahead. I also started to notice not many woman golfers have big breasts. But anyways, golf was a great addition at Fun Towne and stayed popular for decades.

Then Dad added baseball batting cages. Those were tricky to keep in line. The automatic arm that threw the ball would get off balance when wet, resulting in fast wild pitches being thrown at little kids, but kids and baseball guys are resilient. They paid for pitches for many years, and it wasn't until 1999 that the pitching machine finally gave out and the cages were disassembled.

All during the 1980s, Fun Towne roared with go-kart
racing, barroom antics, bowling and golf. The bar was
really the best money maker. Draft beer for 50 cents,
hot dogs steamed in beer and pickled eggs. It was quite
the menu. I grew up behind that bar, and learned a lot
about life, some good, some I'd rather forget. I could
write a whole book on just the bar. The laughs and tears
that were shared on those bar stools were much more
interesting than the one TV channel we got. But until I
was old enough to actually drink at the bar, I hung out
on the other side of Fun Towne, in the arcade. I wasn't
old enough to drink yet, but I could play a mean game of
pinball.

Chapter 11: Arcade Days

The bar only took up 1/2 of the front room that used to be the Circus Towne gift shop. (Circus Towne ashtray, anyone?) There was still plenty of room for more attractions. It was a logical fit to have a few pinball machines at a bowling alley, and Dad found a pinball/video game renting business that would park the games at Fun Towne and split the proceeds, which was all paid in quarters. It was an easy way to have games on the property without having to purchase and maintain them, especially since arcade games were changing fast in the late 70s and 80s.

At first we featured a few pinball machines and the classic "Digger machines" that my mom would fill up with stuffed animals, arrange the prizes just right so they looked easy to grab with the coin operated hook but proved elusive. I watched many families spend ten times as much as the teddy bear costs to win that bear in that grabber game!

But the day it all changed was in July of 1978, Frank, the pinball rental guy, delivered a new game to Fun Towne: Space Invaders. It was the first of its kind: a real video game with a joystick and buttons. It seems antiquated now, but this is during the time when Pong was the cool Atari game played in homes. The day Space Invaders arrived, my world changed. I pretty much spent the rest of that summer in front of that game. My friends and I played it for hours and just watched those little gray dots float on the screen every day. Space invaders was introduced in 1978, and Fun Towne had it; people drove from miles around to play the new video game.

It didn't take long for the pinball machines to be pushed aside to make room for more new video games; PAC Man, Asteroids, Centipede and the first colored video game ever: Galaxian. It was in 1981 that Donkey Kong was released, and I was soon introduced to Mario, who is still jumping barrels today. But Space Invaders revolutionized the arcade. It was the first video game to allow a high score to be saved for future players to see. The game would feature your name at the top of the screen as the latest high score. What a thrill to see your score on top of a screen and saved for others to try and beat it. Space invaders was also the first game to feature a looping sound track. That sound track was stuck in my head all summer. I still hear that sound featured in songs on the radio today. The games only continued to get louder and more colorful each year. I remember a funny pinball machine we had called "Playboy". It featured pictures of girls in bikinis, and every few minutes, it would whistle or say something in a robotic man's voice, like "Hey, Baby". My mom recalls many quiet nights when she'd be working alone, and she would be startled by sexy talking pinball machines. One night it was really quiet, only a couple of customers hanging around, and there was a guy in the bathroom when the talking Playball Pinball says "wanna get lucky", and the customer exited the men's room thinking it was my mom saying cheesy pick-up lines to him.

We all happily changed dollars into quarters to watch visitors have fun for 25 cents. You can tell a lot about a person if you watch how they play an arcade game. Some read all the instructions on how to play first; some just drop the quarter in and just press buttons furiously. Some get angry and kick the machine; some get addicted and play them like casino slot machines, and some players set out to conquer them!

In 1980, one game that was popular was Asteroids. It was pretty simple, one button and a little triangle spaceship on the screen. You pointed the spaceship at the incoming circles that were supposed to be Asteroids, and you press the one and only button repeatedly to explode the Asteroids. It would be totally boring for today's kids, but back then, it was a challenge. The thing about Asteroids is that you start with three spaceships, and you build up more spaceships as you gain points by shooting incoming asteroids. You could go quite a while on one quarter. In fact, we found out just how long.

During that summer, there was one boy, Mike, who loved to play Asteroids. I would watch him play for hours on one or two quarters. He then started playing longer and longer. So by fall, we had to kick him out at closing time, and he would be bummed out because he had built up a bunch of spaceships and points and wanted to keep playing. One quiet Fall Friday night, this kid came in and started playing. I was working the counter and hanging with a couple of friends. My parents were working the bar and without much business that night, they wanted to close up early around 10 pm. Well, this kid was playing strong. He hadn't stopped for hours and asked if he could keep going as long as he could. None of us knew what the high score was on the Asteroids game, or what happens when you reach the end of the game. We talked my parents into closing up and leaving us kids there to let Mike finish the game.

We turned off all the lights outside and all the rest of the games except for the Asteroid game. Mike sat on a stool in front of this arcade game and proceeded to click that button for hours. He continued on past midnight, only taking a quick run to the bathroom. During these quick jaunts, he would leave the machine alone and sacrifice a few spaceships, but he had plenty to spare.

By 2:00 am, he was still going strong, surviving on just soda and popcorn. My friends and I were taking turns sleeping on the bowling alley benches. By 4:00 am, we were amazed and giddy from being up all night. We started to think that Mike was going to set a world's record for playing the longest continuous game of Asteroids. This, of course, is before the Internet. So how is one supposed to find out what the record is at 4:00 am in October in Northern New Hampshire? Somehow we came up with the idea to call the local radio station and let them know what was going on. The DJ answered the call and was enthusiastic about this event happening in the middle of the night. He proceeded to interview us on the phone about this kid playing one video game, non-stop for 11 hours. I guess it was newsworthy enough for our local station, because they sent someone out to do a live broadcast from Fun Towne at 7:00 am Saturday morning. We were all sleepy and giggly; Mike just kept playing that game. He never talked much anyways. He was a quiet kid, but my friends and I were glad to be his PR agents! We chatted away on the radio about the popularity of video games and button pushing techniques. We were on the radio long before my parents even woke up. They had slept through the night and just assumed he had finished playing hours ago! They soon woke up and started rooting for this kid to set the world's record in their arcade! He ended up playing 24 hours when he finally started getting too tired and losing spaceships. That week, he got all sorts of local publicity, but the rest of the world was ahead of us. Kids were playing Asteroids non-stop for days all over the country due to a bug in the game. If you hit the high score of 99990 points, the game would then "flip over" to zero and you keep all your spaceships and keep playing. The developers of the game discovered this after many arcade owners complained of the game being played too long on one quarter. You could literally play all day on one quarter! But that didn't stop us from promoting Mike's feat! It was cool to be a part of that night, and my dad wanted to make the most of the Fun Towne arcade's 15 minutes of fame.

To build on the excitement of video games and Mike's record, my dad sponsored a trip for him to attend a video game tournament in Chicago. These tournaments were popping up around the country, sponsored by Seta or Atari. The tournament Mike competed was for the game Centipede. We got the game at Fun Towne weeks before for him to practice. Mike flew to Chicago with a family friend and competed. He came in the top twenty and quickly realized the video game world was fast moving, and Twin Mountain wasn't in the fast lane.

When Mike brought home his award, we had a party and created more local press about the story. But soon every one fell in love with the new girl in town, Ms. PACman.

The video game industry flourished throughout the country and in Twin Mountain through 1985, and then Mario started entering people's living rooms. The consoles started to become more affordable and you could play all day, for no quarters, and stay in your pajamas. The home console games killed the arcade business. But of course, game guys never quit; they just find a new game. In the 90s, the "redemption" games became popular such as Skee ball, and soon the video games were being pushed aside to bring back Skee ball alleys. Skee Ball never goes out of style.

Chapter 12: My Life is a Circus without the Tent

I graduated from high school in 1983, the era of big everything, including big hair and big boobs; good trends for me! I was a B student and could cruise through classes without breaking a sweat, but none of my classes got me too excited. Honestly, how can school compete with the circus education I was getting? Math was mostly for jocks, science for geeks and English for the nice guys. But I did like typing class. Flash Gordon was the nickname of the popular typing teacher, and it always made me laugh to hear the sounds of those electric typewriters clicking away with students staring at papers on typewriter stands. I picked up typing pretty easily since I had been playing video games for the past four years. Timings were just like challenging my neighbors to a round of Space Invaders. One just needed to focus and move fingers fast. I was a natural.

I also enjoyed accounting; since I had watched my dad and my sisters manage the checkbook at Fun Towne for years. There were actual systems for what my dad was doing in his back office! It really was an epiphany for me that others kept spreadsheets similar to what we used at Fun Towne. So with this background, I decided to major in business administration at a college in Bangor, Maine. But, during the last few months of high school, something appeared in the back room of the business department. The students didn't really know what this white machine was; the teachers said it was a computer. We would turn it on and get a gray screen, but no one knew how to work it, and there wasn't a joy stick. The computer had arrived and I was intrigued.

Not to say that when I left town Twin Mountain turned boring, but that's what I'm going to say. A little tired would be how some people described Twin Mountain during those years. The rise of the chain hotels took a toll on the mom-and-pop motels along the strip. Many of the bars closed, and Fun Towne had to keep with the times. As my dad got older, he changed the attractions at Fun Towne. Go-karts were finished by 1989. Even drinking was getting old and the bar closed down in the early 1990s to make room for more games. Fun Towne was a family attraction with Skee ball machines, mini-golf, video games and the driving range.

My parents finally had enough of the long NH winters and decided to close during the winter months. My dad hung a sign on the door in November that said "gone fishing" and left for Florida with my mom to rent a camper and actually fish for 6 months. It was cheaper for them to go to Florida and just have fun then to work all winter to pay the heating bills. That big, old Fun Towne building cost a fortune to heat, and 50-cent beers just weren't paying the bills anymore.

All of Twin Mountain was trying to find its way in the 1990s. My dad kept picking up golf balls, fixing bowling alley machines, and my mom kept handing out prizes for Skee ball tickets. Skee ball prizes became a real passion for my mom. She enjoyed purchasing the popular items of the day: fake vampire teeth, whoopee cushions and lots of rubber duckies.

I was dabbling in computers while working in administrative jobs in real estate, education, and hospitality. I tried a few different careers and didn't really like working for other people. It seemed odd to work for others, when I had lived in an entrepreneurial atmosphere my whole life. So after I worked at some boring jobs, got married and did some traveling, I started a computer training business. Windows and Word were the new games in town, and since I could figure them out from my experience of arcade games and word processing programs, I could teach others and charge a fee!

In 1996, I took a computer class at a college in Vermont. To communicate with the instructor, I used email for the first time. This amazed me, and I have not stopped emailing since. I quickly took to using AOL, CompuServe, and explored the networks that preceded the web. I saw a new frontier and so did my dad. He kept buying old computers and bringing them to me and asking me to figure out how to use them at Fun Towne. I couldn't do much until the World Wide Web started, and we soon realized how powerful a tool this was for small business owners. The first thing my dad wanted was a website about Twin Mountain. So we bought the domain, TwinMountain.com. I learned some HTML and set up a funky website to promote our town to the rest of the world. The site was popular - it led me to start a web marketing business with my husband, and we've been making websites for local businesses ever since. The web is an exciting place to work. We fight Russians Spammers, Spanish Cybersquatters and work with programmers from all over the world. Yet I can still look out my window at the White Mountains.

Chapter 13: The Show Must Go On

"The show must go on" was a popular phrase in my household growing up. "Smile kid, this is show business", my mom would tell me. Even in Twin Mountain, NH, she was a show business professional! There could be relatives sick in the back room, and her saying was always "smile! The show must go on!" I think that was all my parents said the summer of '74 at Circus Towne when it rained every night at 7 pm.

I could be having a serious boyfriend issue, and it all would be discussed while handing out bowling shoes. "That's awful honey; now go fix the stuck pin in alley 5". It sounds harsh, but dealing with major life issues like divorce or death in front of happy tourists enjoying their mini-golf game isn't so bad. You can't really take life too seriously when watching a goofy guy putt a golf ball in the clown's nose.

My dad passed away at Fun Towne, while it was open for business. It was June – tourist season. He was giving me instructions from his hospital bed on where the supplies were for the golf ball picker upper. During that summer family, friends and many past customers stopped by Fun Towne to pay their respects and share stories. It was heartwarming to hear from all the people who had enjoyed Circus Towne and Fun Towne over the years. We kept the place open that summer after he passed away, and then sold it a few years later to find new adventures. My family still roller skates, has horses, and good times in the White Mountains. And my mom continues to tell me to smile. As they say... the show must go on.

Made in the USA
Middletown, DE
19 October 2022

13028963R00036